THE POWER OF THE "F" WORD IN THE WORKPLACE

THE POWER OF THE "F" WORD IN THE WORKPLACE

Amanda Hill

The Power of the "F" Word in the Workplace

ISBN: 979-8-218-06556-0

Published by: Joseph's Ministry, LLC

www.josephsministryllc.com

Introduction

Written May 14, 2009-

Today is my mommy's birthday. I was okay until one of my sisters called me this morning. It's not just her birthday; I wish she was still here. It is acknowledging that because of this woman's faith, I exist. She looked past all medical understanding, was healed, and gave birth to me. How amazing is she? How amazing am I?

I remember my last birthday with her, my fourth. My oldest sister reminded me of it years ago. We had just left the doctors' office, and my mom received some shocking news, so bad that she didn't tell my older sister. Instead, she told my sister to stop at the store because she wanted to get me something for my birthday. Now understand, my mom had rules, and when she said, "Get what you want," that really meant get one thing, on a good day, maybe two. But this day was different; she said, "Mandy, get whatever you want." So I put one thing in the basket. She said, "No, baby, you get whatever you want." Then, without hesitating, she grabbed everything and put it in the basket. My sister and I were shocked, knowing this behavior was not normal. My mom knew it was her last birthday with me, so she passed the next month.

I live my life now, grabbing everything pure and true, all my desires in my heart, dreams, and visions, and putting them into my basket—claiming and demanding everything I want in life and making it come to pass, living by the same faith which allowed me to exist today.

I sometimes cry, not because I wish to hug her and look into her eyes. I cry because I thank her. For loving me enough, trusting in her God, and teaching me what faith looks like. She has not physically been in my life for all the years, but in only four years, she planted many seeds in my heart when the world tried to kill me; physically, mentally, and spiritually it didn't work. Those seeds were rooted in good ground. They grew into a harvest that would feed millions. It has allowed me to become the woman that I am today.

How do you give thanks to someone for your life? I say it could be by living your life to the highest possible level, a level that you cannot fully understand. And never stop putting things in your basket.

This book represents one of the many things in my basket. As discussed in this book, our childhood and adolescence mold us into the adults we are today. Some can take the bad experiences and mirror them; others can learn, develop and grow from them. With the right mentors, I've learned from my childhood what not to do and what to do.

I've become grateful for my past experiences because, during those times, I was being developed. Through perseverance, I built character. I know I have dreams in my basket that have not come to pass yet, but I believe in my patience. I also believe that by focused, standing with hope, with my eyes on the end goal; not getting distracted by what's in front of me, the understanding of knowing the power of forgiveness; I'm able to welcome the stages of being uncomfortable; and stand, expecting greatness in my future.

Thank you for opening your minds to hear my journey, intending to stretch yourself, learn lessons through my development, and understand how forgiveness and welcoming being uncomfortable in the workplace can change your life and walk you right into your purpose.

Throughout each lesson, you will find discussion questions. These questions allow you to internalize and search deep within yourself with the intent of finding the root cause behind certain behaviors. Feel free to use the notes section at the end of each lesson to write down your thoughts. You can also utilize "The Power of the "F" Word in the workplace journal to guide you throughout each lesson.

Lesson

1

Lesson 1

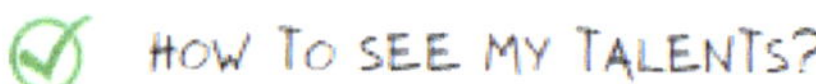

✓ HOW TO SEE MY TALENTS?

✓ HOW LIFE EXPERIENCES EFFECT MY CAREER?

✓ HOW MY COPING MECHANISMS AFFECT MY SURROUNDINGS
AND THE PEOPLE AROUND ME?

I Have Talents Too

For years, I didn't know I had a personal gift, a "talent," as many call it. I would look at everyone around me and see everyone else's gifts but never recognize my own.

I've always been into sports, playing in high school and college; I would say I was talented, but that wasn't my passion, so I didn't put in the extra practice time to become a division one player. I only played if I had to.

I have a distinguished career, and I enjoy building relationships with my stakeholders, especially encouraging them; the funny thing is, I never viewed that as a talent. People would just say, you're natural at it.

I viewed talent as something tangible, something that could be measured. I had a friend who could fix anything; his business card said, "If I can't fix it, it can't be fixed." Seriously, he was so talented; this man could fix anything. Now, I have no desire to fix cars, but like I said, I have the gift of recognizing other people's talents and encouraging them; it comes naturally. Before he got those business cards and his certification as a mechanic, who do you think was encouraging him to pursue what he was talented at? He finished his certification and went on to open his own mechanic shop.

It took me years to identify that my talent was seeing other people's talent and encouraging them to pursue it. I always wondered why I went through so much as a young child and early adulthood, and it was all to develop myself to share with the world how to not give up and how they could pursue their passion. Encouraging is what I do, not by choice, but by default.

Discussion 1.0

YOUR PASSION WILL ALIGN WITH WHAT YOUR NATURAL TALENT IS.

WHAT COMES EASY TO YOU?

____

____

____

Another gift I identified within myself is that I forgive quickly. This caused me trouble, at an immature age, because I assumed the other person had moved on too. Yes, not so much. I forgave quickly because I just wanted to be loved; unfortunately, I interacted with people who loved conditions. I learned this behavior as what love was. If you are doing what people ask of you, I tell you, they will love you back. I became very guarded in my early adulthood because I got hurt very easily, but no one knew that. So I kept that part to myself. As I matured, I continued to forgive, but without expectations. I realized that was the thing that was hurting me, expecting something back in return. I learned that love has nothing to do with conditions, and those weren't the type of people I wanted in my life.

Discussion 1.1

How you react to personal life experiences is what helps shapes your character.

- Can you think of childhood experiences that have shaped your character?

____

____

____

A challenging part about being an encourager and someone who forgives quickly is by knowing when to walk away.

I've been in positions where I had to pump myself up to walk into the company's building. The environment would be so toxic that I would physically get sick. I was in a situation where a supervisor took a project I created, put it on a different document, and put their name on it. I couldn't believe it. Forgiving and encouraging were not on my mind at this time. I was livid. I honestly didn't know what to do. I did know a few things; I was the brain behind this, so if anyone had questions, they would have to come to me. I planned to say nothing.

I thought about this for days. The positive "go get it" attitude had changed, and I lost all motivation. I didn't mention it to anyone; I continued doing my job well and eventually returned to myself. Finally, I decided to let it go and forgive her because I don't think she meant to hurt me in her heart. Months later, I was asked to join another team in a different department, which was a big promotion for me. My former supervisor was happy for me, and we had an opportunity to talk. She was under a lot of stress, personally and professionally, with the company. I did what I do best and encouraged her. We walked away smiling. The next day, another supervisor gave me a phone call informing me that she had passed away. It turns out she had a stroke in her sleep; she is only 34 years old.

I share this story because forgiveness released me from holding on to the chains of my hurt and continued to perform at my highest level, which opened doors to a promotion. It also allowed me to work with an open-minded approach and attitude and understand the innocence within people. Finally, my mind and heart were at peace because the power of the "F" word allowed our relationship to have closure before her untimely passing.

Discussion 1.2

- What if I told people in the company about my feelings towards seeing my work with her name on it?

- What if I didn't forgive her and spoke bad about her to other supervisors before her passing?

Pushing Through Life Experiences

Experiences can help you reach your destiny or prevent you from it. There's power when you realize that experiences are just that, experiences, and they are designed to teach, encourage, empower, guide, and develop you. The challenge with experiences is the journey; often, the development journey can be rough, painful, confusing, and lonely, but at its core, only plain hard.

Sometimes, we forget that everyone has a childhood with experiences. More times than not, our childhoods are not a perfect picture. People have experienced childhood divorces, separation of parents, verbal or physical abuse, rejection, abandonment, and even a death of a parent or sibling. All our childhood experiences form our values and morals within our minds, which are reflected in our daily behavior.

Our childhood experiences continue to follow us, but with different faces.

Let's talk about my friend, Tony. As a child, Tony has an overbearing and controlling mother; she loves to talk and ask questions. Tony wasn't allowed to have sleepovers as a child and had the earliest curfew in high school compared to his other friends. His mother cleaned his room until he left home, but unlike other children, Tony wasn't happy with it and wanted to be more independent. As an adult, he immediately gets angry when he must deal with people with similar behaviors. Tony is dealing with the same issues as he did as a child. However, this time, as an adult, he has the power to speak up and not allow this behavior to overpower him, as it did in his childhood.

The interesting thing is that Tony reacts like he did as a child. Why is that? Because he never dealt with this behavior from the right perspective; instead, he gets irritated and frustrated by the behavior because it reminds him of past experiences, but Tony doesn't even know that's why he gets upset. For example, he still gets irritated with his mother as an adult if she asks too many questions, and he excuses not attending family gatherings.

Let's discuss how Tony's childhood behavior affects Tony in his work life.

Tony gets a new supervisor. This supervisor enjoys talking to his employees and asking loads of questions that can sometimes come across as micromanaging. Tony is immediately stressed out, doesn't want to communicate with the new supervisor, and hates his job now. He believes his supervisor doesn't believe in him because of all the questions and never-ending meetings to monitor his projects. Tony's attitude is negative, and his new supervisor has become negative too, feeding off of Tony. Tony sought advice from other co-workers, who informed him that as soon as they communicated with the new supervisor, they agreed on the way to supply daily updates, the meeting decreased, and they formed a healthy working relationship. However, this communication irritated Tony, and he also stopped talking to that employee.

What is going on here? First, Tony needs to deal with the genuine issues within his heart, which is the relationship between him and his mother. He has unresolved issues from his childhood, which are now showing up in the workplace.

Discussion 1.3

This basic example occurs every day in the workplace. Painfully, sometimes people aren't self-aware to ask themselves hard questions, in order to get to the root of the problem.

- Can you think of specific behaviors that irritate you in the workplace? Try to focus on the behavior, not the person. How do you react to this type of behavior in your workplace?

- Can you think of someone from your past that has this same behavior?

- How do you interact with this person when they demonstrate this behavior, in your personal life?

Picture a child that was rejected and, unfortunately, never dealt with this. Now, as an adult, in the workplace, they're defensive; they feel that they must defend themselves because, at any given moment, someone can come against them and cause them to look bad or lose their job. Just as the example with Tony, this person who battles with rejection will create unnecessary drama within the workplace, as before, unknowingly to them; it's all coming from a familiar pain point.

From a personal point of view, I dealt with abandonment and rejection as a child and in early adulthood. I'd attract similar behaviors from my past because my behavior would act as a magnet. For instance, if I say, "people will let you down," coming from a place of abandonment and rejection, each time someone tries to be friends with me, I'll push them away, creating that reality in my life, "people will let you down."

How do we see this in the workplace? Do you think that maybe the person that doesn't want to be involved may have a fear of being rejected? This is a moment not to judge or assume this person is antisocial; instead, they need time to build trust within the group to open up.

We all have childhood or adolescent issues that need to be resolved. The key is to have self-awareness. As I reflect during my car drives, I often ponder the day and ask myself questions. Did I handle this well? Maybe I could have addressed that email differently. In the core, my reflection is on myself, not my coworkers. I'll ask myself the hard questions: Why does my co-worker's behavior bother me? This is the true power of self-reflection. If I'm honest, I'll find the root of the answer within myself.

I'll share another personal example with you. I was going through a nasty divorce, and no one within my company would have ever known, other than a few who noticed me not wearing my ring. I didn't take any time off work. Instead, I handled my business, cried when needed, talked about it with close and honest friends, and kept it moving. I sought counseling and didn't allow that experience to hinder me from growth and development. Now, should I assume or expect everyone else in my situation to follow suit? If they ask for time off, are they less of a person or "weak"? Absolutely not! We must understand that we're all different based on our different childhood experiences.

I learned one rule that worked for me throughout my life and used it here. It is the power of the "F" word. I forgave and used it as fuel to keep me pushing through and provided an example to my daughter. I became more loving towards people, more forgiving, and more understanding. Why? It is because that is what I needed during this time in my life. I became a magnet to what I needed and rejected what I didn't need.

With that said, when people got under my skin at work during this season, instead of getting pissed off, I smiled and offered my services. I would go out of my way to not become bitter or upset. Instead, I practiced the "F" word, Forgiveness. My environment changed on all levels due to self-awareness. People ask me today, how did you get through this? I did it because I knew the effects of stress on my life and chose to forgive from my core.

Like many people, I don't handle stress well. I get very skinny, sick and lethargic. With this understanding, I refuse to be stressed. I had responsibilities with my daughter and my toddler nephew to care for independently, and I needed my health and strength. I decided that stressing was not part of the plan. I had an opportunity to react as I did during my childhood by feeling rejected and abandoned, but I couldn't because I forgave my past and chose to forgive my present. I know that's why I continued to progress in my company because I refused to allow this experience of getting a divorce to stop me from developing. I had focused on the end result, not the experience in front of me.

Discussion 1.4

Can you think of a personal life changing event, where you had to choose to push through, and not allow it to stop you from reaching your goal?

____

____

____

How Coping Affects the People around You

When I was in college, I would suffer from severe hives. I'll never forget waking up in the middle of the night with hives all over my body, getting rushed to the ER by friends and the ER doctor looking right into my eyes and saying, "I don't know what you're going through, but whatever it is, let it go. You couldn't have woken up." He gave me a shot in my arm, and from that day forward, I never had another hive attack. I made a choice that my health was more important than stress.

We all have stress in our lives and handle it based on our life experiences. How you deal with stress is so important, and some people prefer not to deal with stress at all. In my opinion, that's when your body deals with it for you. You're displacing it somehow, affecting the people around you.

The statistics below come from The National Institute for Occupational Safety and Health (NIOSH) Digesting the Statistics of Workplace Stress.

The National Institute for Occupational Safety and Health (NIOSH) is the Federal agency responsible for conducting research and making recommendations for the prevention of work-related illness and injury. NIOSH is part of the U.S. Department of Health and Human Services; it is distinct from the Occupational Safety and Health Administration (OSHA), a regulatory agency located in the U.S. Department of Labor.

"Numerous surveys and studies confirm that occupational pressures and fears are far and away the leading source of stress for American adults and that these have steadily increased over the past few decades. While there are tons of statistics to support these allegations, how significant they are, depends on such things as how

the information was obtained (self-report vs. answers to carefully worded questions), the size and demographics of the targeted group, and how participants were selected and who sponsored the study. Some self-serving polls claiming that a particular occupation is "the most stressful" are conducted by unions or organizations to get higher wages or better benefits for their members. Others may be conducted to promote a product, such as the "Stress in the Nineties" survey by the maker of a deodorant that found housewives were under more stress than the CEOs of major corporations. Such a conclusion might be anticipated from telephone calls to residential phones conducted in the afternoon. When evaluating job stress statistics, it is crucial to remember all these caveats."
https://www.stress.org/workplace-stress/

Reflect on the graphs below for the "main cause of stress" in your workplace.

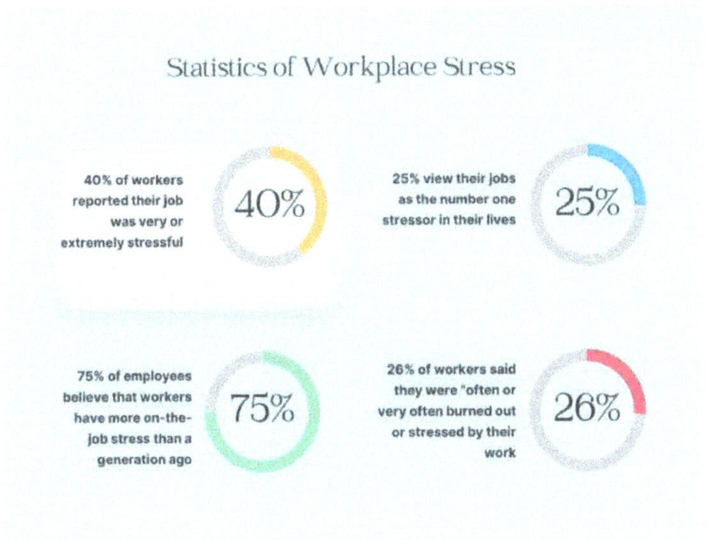

Statistics of Workplace Stress

80% of workers feel stress on the job, nearly half say they need help in learning how to manage stress and 42% say their coworkers need such help

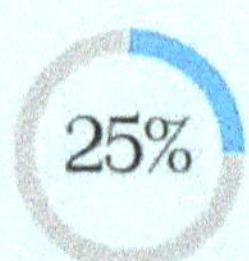

25% have felt like screaming or shouting because of job stress, 10% are concerned about an individual at work they fear could become violent

14% of respondents had felt like striking a coworker in the past year, but didn't.

9% are aware of an assault or violent act in their workplace and 18% had experienced some sort of threat or verbal intimidation in the past year

Statistics of Workplace Stress

65% of workers said that workplace stress had caused difficulties and more than 10 percent described these as having major effects

10% said they work in an atmosphere where physical violence has occurred because of job stress and in this group

42% report that yelling and other verbal abuse is common

29% had yelled at co-workers because of workplace stress

14% said they work where machinery or equipment has been damaged because of workplace rage

Discussion 1.5

- What keeps you up at night?

- How do you deal with stress?

- Would you consider it healthy?

- What if I asked you to do the best you can, with whatever it is and let it go?

- For some people the idea of "letting go", the thought alone brings them stress.

- How is stressing out about a task helping you get to the goal faster?

- Can you think of another way to handle high pressure situations?

I can only change myself, so why put the focus on anyone else? My behavior will affect others, and I can create a stressful environment for myself and others through either my reaction or my responses. Responding and reacting to situations are distinctively different and unique. Responding is taking the situation in and deciding the best course of action based on values and principles, really thinking about the act. Reacting is usually your 'gut feeling,' the first act toward a situation is often based on fear and insecurities.

People will worry themselves into a frantic state, and nothing good comes from worry. Being concerned and worrying are two different things. Personal example - If I'm concerned about my daughter, I'll call her and make sure I know her whereabouts, communicate my concerns and end the phone call in peace. If I'm worried about her, I'm thinking of all the possible negative things that could go wrong, can't focus on what's in front of me, and talk about the situation repeatedly with no peace. See the difference?

When you're a worrier, you take it everywhere you go, especially in the workplace. The difficult thing about bringing it into the workplace is that you don't have all the control, and more times than not, you must rely on another person and department, which will only create unnecessary stress.

Discussion 1.6

Based off of the feedback above, 80% of workers feel stress on the job, nearly half say they need help in learning how to manage stress, and 42% say their coworkers need such help.

- How do you handle your stress level at work?

- Where does your stress level fall on a scale of 1 to 10?

Notes

Lesson 2

Lesson 2
GETTING USED TO BEING UNCOMFORTABLE

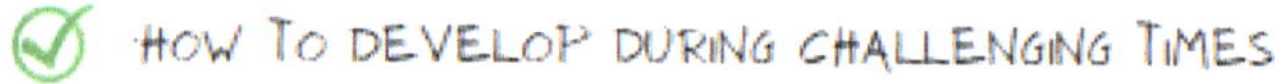

✓ HOW TO DEVELOP DURING CHALLENGING TIMES

✓ EMOTIONAL FULFILLMENT

✓ DOWNFALLS TO EMOTIONAL FULFILLMENT

In 2006, I started living my life stronger physically, mentally, and spiritually. Making all three a priority in my life, for years, one out of the three has always been absent. In 2006, I was preparing for my first figure competition, the Heart of Texas. I discovered my passion, living a healthy life and encouraging others to do the same. At first, it was just a thought; "Let's see what my body will look like if I really push it to the limit." It was supposed to be only a physical challenge, but it turned out to be much greater than that. It changed me physically, but more mentally and spiritually.

Some may be thinking, "mentally and spiritually, how so? Please understand that when you're trying to accomplish anything in life, it can be something as small as cleaning up your house, as large as trying to lose 100 pounds, or getting that promotion at your job; distractions and obstacles are always going to be present. The key is to know how to conquer and overcome those obstacles.

I've noticed that distractions come when I'm trying to focus on something new, and like clockwork, a small life event happens, which allows me to use it as my scapegoat. I know no one has ever done this before, using their kids or pets as an excuse to get out of doing something. For fun, let's say I've been working out to lose 20 pounds. I'm three weeks in and sore all over. I'm just about to start my workout when I get a phone call that my child is ill at school, and I must pick them up. I stop what I'm doing and head out to the school. Instead of preparing a meal at home, I stop and get something to go, which is not on the healthy side. I tell myself it's for my child; it'll make them feel better. I managed to get something for myself. After I get my child settled, I decide not to workout at home, and the equipment has now become a coat rack. I tell myself it is okay; I need a break. I'll get going tomorrow.

The next day, I'm invited to happy hour after work. Sure, why not? Each day comes and goes. I'm back in my comfort zone with no exercise or healthy choices, but something in me isn't happy. I may have felt comfortable doing what was familiar and not stretching myself, but on the inside, I wanted more. The problem was I didn't know how to become different or something greater than my current situation, mainly because being uncomfortable is not an easy place to live.

How to Develop During Challenging Times

Being uncomfortable does not feel good. However, to grow, we have to be in an uncomfortable state. Muscles build by tearing down and building back up. The building backup process is painful; that's what we call "sore." If you stop the pain, you've stopped the growing process. This principle is true in every area of our life.

Cultural changes are exciting for some people and terrifying for others. Change means new processes, new management, new ideas, etc. For some people, this is stressful. They think about layoffs, learning a new system, and a different supervisor that may not support them. Yet, change is a chance to embrace it and develop yourself. Unfortunately, many people don't see it that way. Instead, they focus on the negative whispers, which distract them from seeing the truth and growth within the development process.

Let's talk about my friend, Brad, who had a great position in the world of Information Technology. He was one of the top company employees well educated. His work spoke for itself. He was informed that the company would be having some layoffs soon, but would they give him a month's notice, and it wouldn't take place for at least six months? He immediately went into panic mode. He moved out of his apartment and back in with his parents; Brad was a nervous wreck and got physically ill. Brad forgot his talents and focused on his life experiences in front of him. The good news, Brad surrounds himself with wise friends and family. They reinforced what was already in him by reminding him of his talents and giving sound advice. Subsequently, Brad applied for a higher position within another company. He was called in for an interview and was hired on the spot. This happened within two weeks of hearing the news about layoffs. His new position paid more; with better benefits and hours, came with a higher title; and the best part is, his responsibilities were the same as his previous job, with the help of his social circle. This stage of being uncomfortable pushed him to believe in his talents and pursue a career greater than before. He almost got caught in the experience and lost focus; however, he believed in his talents and allowed the moment to move him into a better position.

I heard once that you couldn't control the birds from flying over your head, but you can stop them from building a nest on it. I look at these "birds" as the distractions we all encounter daily. Have you ever noticed a group of birds dancing in the sky? It's so interesting that they can draw your full attention. You get lost in time as they gracefully move in sequence in the sky to an unknown tone. Distractions do this; they amuse us or cause us to lose focus on what is truly important. They camouflage themselves as the priority when it's just white noise.

Throughout life, we've all heard of dreams never coming to pass. Life passions are never pursued due to unexplained obstacles out of their control. This person hit a barrier and just didn't know or have the tools to get around it, which prevented them from accomplishing their dreams or not becoming all, they were sent here to be. This "change" in this stage of being uncomfortable is here to push you out of your comfort zone to grow you to the place you need to be, to be prepared for your ultimate passion.

Discussion 2.0

- From a scale of 1 to 10, how easily are you distracted with life experiences, that in turn, affects you in the workplace?

____

____

____

Emotional Fulfillment

We are all guilty of taking the easy way out. Especially when we're in a place stretching us mentally, repeating a cycle where the end results aren't producing value or substance based on the original intent can lead one into a place of regret and frustration. "Stretching" moments are when you have to see past what's in front of you to get to your destination. During these times, we tend to push back and run towards what's familiar: a place of physical fulfillment. Unfortunately, these places we go to often don't progress us toward our goal; instead, that place pulls us back. This stage is what I call my "plateau," nothing productive happens here. I get to do all the things that make my physical body feel good, and in this place, I justify all my actions because the development is too much, so I tell myself.

Who really wants to push toward pain and get to the other side? We all do, but it's painful. Let's be honest; it doesn't feel good. If you aim to get another degree or certification, you have to be determined and not get distracted by life. Life will come in and tell you that you don't have time for this, you can't lose any weight, you're not qualified for that promotion, you don't have the money to start a new business, and no one will listen to your ideas. Life happens. But so do dreams.

What if Bill Gates with Microsoft, Oprah Winfrey with the OWN network, and Steve Jobs with his vision of Apple, all decided to follow their emotional fulfillment and no longer battle with people or life and just live a regular life? You see, falling towards comfort is easy, but pushing through the uncomfortable zone is where dreams come true, and passions are developed.

For a moment, go back to a time when you had a personal goal and didn't achieve it, something that you were passionate about. Did you want to go back to school, lose 20 pounds, start a new business, or even de-cluttering your house? Believe it or not, we all hit a moment while reaching our goal, a   moment where we must decide to battle through a storm or retreat under pressure. I call this moment the "uncomfortable zone."

Let me discuss Kevin; he dreams of opening a unique coffee café in his small town with a population of around 10,000. Looking at him, you would never believe he was a coffee connoisseur. He works in a small warehouse, is married with one child, and loves the smell of freshly brewed coffee. Kevin was born in America but raised by his grandparents in Jamaica until the age of 16, when he moved back to America with his mother.

Kevin has a dream and started putting together the plan to make it happen. He's now 42, and for the last 20 years, he's been adding $200 away bi-weekly into a compound interest account, earning him a great interest rate annually to the dollar. Today, Kevin has more than enough to open his store. He found the perfect location, a small storefront right in the heart of their downtown.

He was months away from getting all his products and the store together when something unspeakable happened. His wife of 15 years was in an awful car accident. This rocked Kevin's world. Kevin did not have the best health insurance, and the medical bills were piling up. Before he knew it, Kevin had used more than half of his savings for the store towards his wife's medical bills.

Kevin was on the edge of smoking cigarettes again to help relieve the stress. Years ago, he stopped smoking by looking at the money he spent and decided to invest it instead of smoking it. Instead of picking up a cigarette, he exercised at home when his wife was resting. A month later, his wife returned home, and he's extremely grateful. Yet, a small part of him is disappointed. He was so close to his dream, and now it seems unreachable. His wife and friends are concerned because he's not the same anymore. Although he was months away from quitting the warehouse and walking into his dream, he said to his wife one night, "Maybe it wasn't meant for us to open a coffee shop; maybe that money was being saved to help us during this time of need." Kevin has given up and now doubting his dream. His wife immediately stops him in his tracks and begins to encourage and remind him of his hard work and dreams. Kevin's wife healed sooner than expected, and they were able to start saving again.

This story didn't end there; Six months later, Kevin got a call from an attorney in Jamaica; apparently, his grandfather had passed away; he had an account with over $100,000. Now guess whose name was on it? That's right, Kevin. Kevin was able to open up his dream coffee shop after all. One might think it was happenstance when the money came in. Others may think it was the power of his thought life. You can say that Kevin chose to see life from the best point of view possible and surround his life with positive people who supported him emotionally.

Here's another story that's not so extreme. My friend Jordan was an hourly employee for a large company. He earned his Green Belt in Six Sigma and was praying for a salary position, and he earned one as Business Analysis. This was an amid-level position; however, the salary was more than he had earned in the past. He was finally earning a nice salary and in a position that really challenged him, and he loved his team.

In Jordan's new position, he had to interact with a remote office, with a sarcastic supervisor who was not tactful with words.

Jordan was okay initially because the lead Business Analyst would deal with this supervisor most of the time. One day, his lead Business Analyst received a promotion and was going to leave the department. Jordan knew he would be the first in line now to deal with the remote supervisor. Jordan physically got ill from the stress. He reached out to his old lead asking for advice, and each time, he was told not to give up, to keep communicating, don't quit and lose his tender with the company over one person, and to believe in himself because it would get better over time.

After one month, Jordan couldn't handle the pressure and left the company. He didn't leave for a better-paying job; he left because of the stress and went to a less challenging job. He would rather make less money than continue with the fear of making mistakes and getting ridiculed.

Three weeks later, that supervisor was moved to a different line of business; if Jordan had stayed, he would've no longer worked with this person. When Jordan found out, he was so disappointed in his decision. To make matters worse, he left the company without notice and can't return.

Now, these two stories are different, and Kevin's example is extreme; however, the principle is the same as Jordan's. We all have dreams or passions we want to achieve. We can plan each moment, each step, and think it's all in alignment, and out of nowhere, life can happen. This is the "uncomfortable zone" this is where a storm of life comes to distract or prevents us from moving forward. This is where we must make the hard choice to push through, win, accept our position and possibly give up on our passion.

Discussion 2.1

- Have you ever dreamt of something big or had a passion for a different lifestyle and "life" happen?

- How did you handle this? Did you continue to pursue it?

____

____

____

____

____

____

____

GOAL TIMELINE

In the illustration above, the first graph demonstrates a perfect world. You set a goal, and you achieve it without any distractions or hiccups. But unfortunately, the real world is more like the "uncomfortable zone" design above.

You're full of passion and excitement and decide to set a goal to achieve what's unknown to you. Unknowingly, let's say your dream will come to life in 6 months. During these six months, "life happens," and you must decide to persevere or give up. This is where we normally turn to emotional fulfillment. For some, it may be overeating, spending money they don't have, unhealthy relationships, and partaking in too much partying or drinking. We all have the vices we run to.

A way to overcome leaning on unhealthy choices is to surround yourself with great friends or family who are there to support and encourage you through the good and bad without any personal motives. They will remind you of who you are and not allow you to forget your passion. If you don't have these types of people in your corner, find them. Join groups with like-minded people and honor them as they honor you.

If you fall under "emotional fulfillment" and can't find your way back to your target, depression may creep in. Depression is a sneaky one; a lot of times, you don't even know you're depressed until it's too late. You can start having a significant increase or decrease in appetite and time spent sleeping, feelings of dejection, and hopelessness; these are all symptoms of depression.

In the "uncomfortable zone" timeline, depression comes after emotional fulfillment; that's not coincidental. After you buy something, drink something, eat something, smoke something… you get the idea. Reality kicks in, and you start remembering the storm that came that prevented you or distracted you from reaching your goal and start kicking yourself or blaming someone else.

Let's talk briefly about the "fear" point in the timeline, within the "uncomfortable zone." When you're blaming yourself or the people around you just to justify your decision negatively, that's a sign that fear is in the mix. Fear is a reaction to the unseen future. It's based on a bit of truth, but its focus is on something that isn't guaranteed in the future. Fear comes, so you don't see the truth; instead, you focus on all the distractions. Use Jordan's story as an example; he had a fear of the unknown. Yes, there was an unprofessional person he had to deal with; however, this was not his direct supervisor, and therefore, he had no control over his future within the company. Instead, Jordan allowed fear to come in and create anxiety and panic.

For example, we said the goal unknowingly would come to pass in 6 months if you continue to persevere. However, many people don't stay on target and question their original goals or dream. You will hear things like, "maybe it wasn't my time," or I really didn't want to do that anyway. You allow your thoughts of fear, depression, blame, or shame to lead the conversation. Instead, change the narrative. Try saying, "my day is coming," I'm learning more and more with each day to help me reach my goal. I am successful. I am a leader. I am an overcomer. This is just the beginning." Your thoughts, just like our example story with Kevin, play a role in your future behavior. What and who you listen to will create thoughts, which will turn into words, and in turn, will form your actions and over time turn your behavior into habits. Your goal is to form good habits to help you reach your goals, not hinder them.

Downfalls to Emotional Fulfillment

Forgiveness plays a huge part in our choices regarding emotional fulfillment. I had a coworker who was a chronic smoker. This was his way of relieving stress. He would easily go through a pack a day. He was temporarily relieving his stress but permanently destroying his body. Although, for twenty years, he used smoking to emotionally fulfill his needs; at age 55, he died from heart disease. He had a massive heart attack.

Eating can also be an escape for many people, which can open up the door for depression. In addition, gaining weight can affect your self-image, and overeating can also lead to health problems such as diabetes and heart disease.

Anything emotional is normally geared away from reason. It's based on a state of mind deriving from one's circumstances or mood. Emotions can change like the wind, which is dangerous if you're moving off your emotions. With this understanding, when you're growing 100% of the time, you're going to be developed, and with development comes stages of being uncomfortable. As we discussed, many people run from being uncomfortable and turn to emotional fulfillment, which is a distraction from the long-term goal. If you don't learn how to handle development moments, you'll continue a terrible cycle of never completing your goals. The challenges will continue until you change your reactions to them.

This leads to the difference between self-control and controlling your feelings. I was always taught to practice self-control. That looked like not saying what's "really" on my mind to me—not jumping across the table when someone blatantly disrespects you. I believe in healthy behavior. However, something no one ever taught me was how to control my "inner feelings." Even though I didn't slap her or "tell her how I really felt," the inner feelings are still real, and inside, I'm having all sorts of "unhealthy conversations." Guess what? My body and mind do not know the difference. My body is keeping score. The adrenaline and cortisol are on a high as if it's happening in "real life." Physically I may have a headache, start to sweat, or maybe shake my leg unconsciously. So how do I control my feelings? I will say it's not easy and takes practice, just as mastering external actions took time. Remember all the talks you may have had in elementary school, "keep your hands to yourself"?

Here are a few tips for controlling your feelings.

- Focus on what you want, not what's in front of you.
- Feelings change like the wind. So as soon as another event happens, your feelings will change too.
- Remember, what you're feeling is temporary unless you focus on it.
- Your unconscious mind rules your conscious actions. Meditate on what you want, not what you don't want.
- What you think about is how you will feel, and it will create your language

Unhealthy emotional fulfillment brings about unhealthy consequences. Below are some facts on heart disease, the leading cause of death in both men and women.

FACTS ON HEART DISEASE

RISK FACTORS

High blood pressure, high LDL cholesterol, and smoking are key heart disease risk factors for heart disease. About half of Americans (49%) have at least, one of these three risk factors. Five several other medical conditions and lifestyle choices can also put people at a higher risk for heart disease, including

- Diabetes
- Overweight and obesity
- Poor diet
- Physical inactivity
- Excessive alcohol use

HEART DISEASE IS THE LEADING CAUSE OF DEATH FOR MEN, WOMEN, AND PEOPLE OF MOST RACIAL AND ETHNIC GROUPS IN THE UNITED STATES. ONE PERSON DIES EVERY 34 SECONDS IN THE UNITED STATES FROM CARDIOVASCULAR DISEASE.

About 697,000 people in the United States died from heart disease in 2020–that's 1 in every 5 deaths.

Heart disease cost the United States about $229 billion each year from 2017 to 2018.3 This includes the cost of health care services, medicines, and lost productivity due to death.

Coronary Artery Disease

In 2020, about 2 in 10 deaths from CAD happen in adults less than 65 years old.

In the United States, someone has a heart attack every 40 seconds.

Every year, about 805,000 people in the United States have a heart attack.

Of these, 605,000 are a first heart attack 200,000 happen to people who have already had a heart attack.

About 1 in 5 heart attacks are silent–the damage is done, but the person is not aware of it.

https://www.cdc.gov/dhdsp/data_statistics/fact_sheets/fs_heart_disease.htm

RISK FACTORS

Your lifestyle choices can increase your risk for stroke. The good news is that healthy behaviors can lower your risk for stroke.

Talk with your health care team about making changes to your lifestyle. Eating a diet high in saturated fats, trans fat, and cholesterol has been linked to stroke and related conditions, such as heart disease. Also, getting too much salt (sodium) in the diet can raise blood pressure levels.

Not getting enough physical activity can lead to other health conditions that can raise the risk for stroke. These health conditions include obesity, high blood pressure, high cholesterol, and diabetes. Regular physical activity can lower your chances for stroke.

DRINKING TOO MUCH ALCOHOL CAN RAISE BLOOD PRESSURE LEVELS AND THE RISK FOR STROKE. IT ALSO INCREASES LEVELS OF TRIGLYCERIDES, A FORM OF FAT IN YOUR BLOOD THAT CAN HARDEN YOUR ARTERIES

- Women should have no more than one drink a day.
- Men should have no more than two drinks a day.
- Tobacco use increases the risk for stroke.
- Cigarette smoking can damage the heart and blood vessels, increasing your risk for stroke.
- Nicotine raises blood pressure.

Carbon monoxide from cigarette smoke reduces the amount of oxygen that your blood can carry.

Exposure to secondhand smoke can make you more likely to have a stroke.

https://www.cdc.gov/stroke/risk_factors.htm

Leading Causes of Death in US 2022

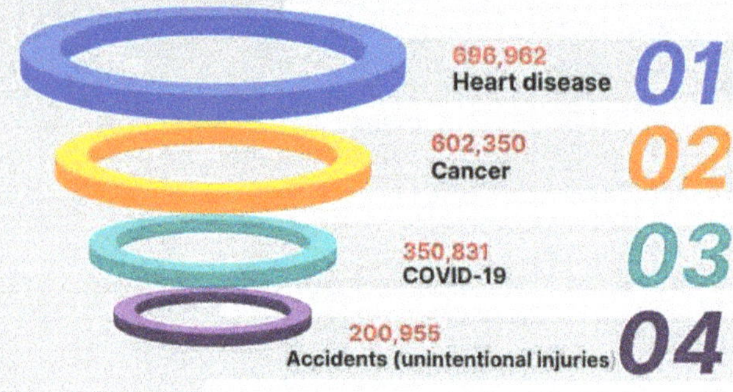

Discussion 2.2

- What emotional fulfillment gives you your "temporary fix"?

- Can you think of a healthy way to get pass stressful moments?

- Do you have a hard time controlling your feelings or lacking self-control?

- Based off of the statistics above are at risk of any health issues or feel as if you need to life a healthier lifestyle?

____

____

____

____

____

____

Notes

Lesson

3

Lesson 3

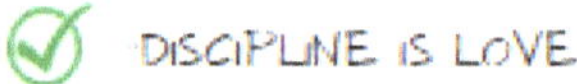

Do I need discipline?

Do I need discipline to reach my goal? I think the better question is can you live without it? Unfortunately, the word "discipline" has a bad reputation. When most people think of discipline, their minds immediately close and think of punishment or correction when it's not that at all. In fact, discipline is self-control, and I believe everyone can use and can benefit from self-control.

When you're teaching a young child, we have healthy guidelines. For example, we don't allow a child to touch a hot stove, run across the street without looking, or eat ice cream all day. Creating discipline at the core is healthy and life-changing.

Structure: Creating structure allows for faster decision-making and improves focus, organization, and productivity, which creates peace during times of stress. Life happens, and having a plan allows you to pivot and not get caught up in the daily hustles of life. Having discipline creates peace.

Results: Execution is the key. We must first put a plan in place and execute it to reach any goal. Having the discipline to create structure in your life isn't always easy, but it will equal results. If you are trying to accomplish something as small as completing the exercise of washing, folding, hanging, and putting away your laundry within the same day or as large as starting a new business – discipline is at the core of it.

Freedom: Saying no to things you "want" allows you to live with less stress. Adding structure and discipline around your money allows for more freedom; for example, going on a trip already paid for, with a budget to enjoy yourself, and returning home with all your household bills and responsibilities handled is freedom. Procrastinating does the complete opposite. Think of you procrastinating on a project, paying a bill, or leaving at the last minute. What do you remember feeling like? Anxious, stressed, rushed, maybe disappointed? Introducing discipline to your lifestyle creates independence and opens areas for more freedom. Carving out time to do what you enjoy is an important part of life. This is another example of using discipline to create time for friends and family without feeling as if your life only consists of working and household duties.

Love: Creating healthy boundaries is a form of self-love. Limitations and guidelines are a great thing. We all know of someone who isn't self-aware and could care less about others' personal space. It's always awkward or uncomfortable to be around someone who doesn't see how their behavior affects the people around them, right? What if you can't see how your own behavior is affecting your own life? Are you limiting yourself by not creating boundaries? Do you lack self-control which results in repeating unhealthy circumstances? To stop repeating unhealthy patterns, you must decide to change your mindset and add some discipline to your life.

How does discipline play a role in forgiveness? The same way you set a goal and create structure to get results is the same way you can create healthy boundaries, which is vital when working towards forgiving someone and yourself.

Obedience equals discipline

Unhealthy: Identifying unhealthy behavior isn't as easy as it sounds unless you have already done the work. What's unhealthy to one may be normal to another. For example, you may have grown up in a house where sarcasm and passive aggression is the norm, so as an adult, you express your frustration in this way. This is very rude and insensitive to another person because that wasn't their norm. Unless you research, you don't know why being sarcastic and passive aggression isn't healthy. Passive aggressive behavior is indirect attacks that can be more exasperating than direct ones. Another reason passive-aggressive behavior is so harmful is that the behavior is so indirect you may think the problem is with you. Whether sarcasm is a sign of intelligence, communication experts and marriage counselors advise us to avoid this expression.

The reason is simple: sarcasm expresses the poisonous sting of contempt, hurting others and harming relationships. Trying to change learned behavior is not easy, to put it plainly; it's simply hard. Most people don't want to do the work and will pass the behavior down from generation to generation. But, those who are up for the challenge and want to change will reap great benefits for not only themselves but their friends and family. To change the pattern, you must identify the behavior, track it back to the root, let it go, and replace it with new behavior.

Healthy: Learning healthy behavior is not as easy as it sounds. You mirror your environment, and you must try to seek a new environment of people, therapy and close friends and family you admire to become. Read books to provide tips on changing your mindset that focuses on your area of interest. Once you get the corrective behaviors be intentional and practice it all day. Accountability partners are key and strongly suggested to grow and learn more about yourself.

Replacing: It is good to learn a new behavior to create new patterns and the process is exciting. The key is not to give up if you fall back to familiar habits. Instead, acknowledge the mistake, ask for forgiveness, and more importantly, forgive yourself. Being intentional and being present to hear what others say is important because we all have blind spots, and we need people around us to keep us on track. This is where discipline kicks in by creating a plan and executing it.

Let's take a basic example: procrastination.

Learned behavior: I watched my parents wait until the last minute to pay bills because they used the money to have fun with us, shopping, sports, etc. I didn't know that it increased stress in their marriage, which resulted in a divorce.

New behavior: I budget accordingly and pay bills on time to prevent additional stress.

Replacing the behavior: Trade procrastination with a structured plan. Creating a plan and structure to develop a routine.

Discussion 3.0

- List one area in your life where you need structure.

- What results are you currently getting in this area?

- Do you see a pattern of bad outcomes in this area?

- Where do you need more freedom in your life?

- Where you add more discipline to create those areas of freedom?

- Do you create healthy boundaries in your life to eliminate confusion or chaos in your life?

- When you do you need to create more healthy boundaries?

____

____

____

____

____

Unlearn chaos

Chaos. The dictionary defines chaos as - complete disorder and confusion. Take a moment to think about what area in your life may have complete disorder and confusion. How is your money management, personal relationships, career, or eating habits? Let's think about our inner selves. How is your self-esteem? Do you practice self-control or live on the edge? Do you have a lot of drama in your life; meaning do you always have a story to tell? Chaos is the opposite of order and without order there is no structure. Living a life of confusion creates more confusion. The challenge with having a lifestyle full of drama is that it can be mistaken as excitement or spontaneous. You can have order and still experience excitement and spontaneity but without stress and dysfunction.

Dysfunction. According to a Forbes article written in 2021 titled "What Does Having A "Real" Family Mean?" – it states recent statistics of, 70%-80% of Americans consider their families dysfunctional. We all have some type of childhood or adolescent issue that impacts us as adults. As a child, you didn't have a choice regarding your surroundings. The great news is that you do now as an adult. If you can track the dysfunctional pattern, you can unlearn it too. Living in what's familiar is easy and doesn't call for change. Stepping out of the norm and doing what's uncomfortable creates change. Learning the difference between a healthy environment and a dysfunctional one is key to reaching your goals because who you surround yourself around will impact your end results.

Order. Order goes hand in hand with structure and discipline. If having order is not familiar to you as a child; it may be difficult to receive it as an adult, because you will feel uncomfortable and maybe like you're in a box. What you don't know is that creating order is allowing you to have a bigger box. How? Order allows you to see all angles of what you're trying to accomplish. It lets you see areas that can be improved and when life events occur you can plan more efficiently without feeling out of control or making an emotional decision instead of a logical plan.

Peace. Don't mistake peace as boredom. Peace allows you to create, focus, dream, manifest your vision and make sound decisions. Think about what peace looks like to you and do you have enough of it? Peace does not operate in confusion or drama. Even during uncertain times, you can still have moments of peace. Allow your brain to stop trying to "figure it out" and let go. This may be a challenge for many especially if you're a control freak but letting go is a key component to receiving peace during trying times.

Forgiveness work is not for the light-hearted. As you're doing the work of unlearning behavior you can slip into blaming others and becoming the victim of "why me". Be careful. Our parents, grandparents or whomever guardians help to raise you did the best they knew to do at the time. Behavior is demonstrated and so often parents aren't aware of how their simple actions and expressions mold their children. Childhood development studies as determined a child as early as 8 months begin to imitate the people around them. Our life should be a cycle of learn, unlearn, and learning.

Discussion 3.1

- What area of your childhood do you feel were dysfunctional?

- Do you see any patterns in your current life that mirrors your childhood experience?

- Do you find it hard to create order in your current life? What steps can you take to add order in your life?

- When you think back to your childhood do you see where chaotic behavior was demonstrated?

- Do you tend to react in the workplace in a similar matter?

____

____

____

____

____

Notes

Lesson 4

Lesson 4

✅ THE POWER OF FORGIVENESS

✅ LEADING BY EXAMPLE

✅ EFFECTS FROM NOT FORGIVING

I have the privilege to teach at an anger management class. Interestingly, there are people from all walks of life with one common denominator: unforgiveness. After they demonstrate no self-control, which is a by-product of something else. We get to the root and ultimately determine that they've been hurt and can't effectively communicate their pain, which results in rage. These men all had goals and dreams but allowed their emotions to control them, destroying potential opportunities for success.

The Power of Forgiveness

In the workplace, I have seen people rage with another coworker to the point of yelling across a room. I've read of people physically fighting each other, sabotaging coworkers in hopes of getting fired, and, sadly, even taking another person's life. These are extreme cases but very true. We never know how someone's childhood developed them as an adult and what will bring them over the edge.

Forgiveness is the cure for it all, and all forgiveness is self-forgiveness.

Let's discuss Tony's example from lesson 1. We explained how because of his childhood with his mother helped mold him as an adult. Now, whenever he's around similar behaviors, he's instantly frustrated and irritated. People within his department shared their experience with the supervisor, and after communicating with them, he still didn't want to deal with it. Tony doesn't know how to forgive; because of this behavior, he could make an emotional decision, react the wrong way, and lose his job.

Imagine Tony getting an epiphany moment and connecting the dots. He has the conversation with his mother, or, better yet, with himself, and let's go of the past and forgives.

The next time he deals with his supervisor, his perception and perspective will be a complete 180.

Never take what happens at the workplace personally. Even if it's said directly to you, as we discussed, people look through a lens based on their own experiences. Everyone is not self-aware. They have their personal goals they are trying to reach within the company; it's never about you.

We have to remember the bottom line in business which is revenue. Without revenue, there is no business. Have successful companies mastered the importance of understanding that their employees and customers come first, and the money will come? Absolutely! Within those companies are still people, and with people comes life experiences that can either hinder or catapult your development; it's up to you to determine the path it takes.

In the story I shared about my old supervisor, I had an opportunity to hold on to being disappointed by her actions and telling others about it. That could have hindered my promotion. When we're hurt, we often want to tell someone so that someone can empathize with us. I'm so grateful I didn't. I had great mentors who taught me the importance of seeing the innocence in a person and letting go.

If I had spoken ill words against her, it would have potentially ruined my reputation, and I would've missed a great movement of development. On a deeper level, knowing we were at a good place added peace to my heart after her passing.

Let's touch on Brad's scenario. Brad could have moved his focus on hating his company for making poor financial decisions and in his mind, "putting him" in this situation. He easily could have taken it personally and allowed it to consume him. He would've become paralyzed in the experience; instead, he chose to let go and pushed forward. In turn, moving him into a better position.

Lead by Example

As a leader, you can't function in a place of holding grudges. People make mistakes; that's life. People tend to look out for themselves and can be opportunists in high-pressure situations. A leader must lead by example and what better way to show leadership than to forgive? Employees will fear making mistakes if they know you can't look past mistakes. Encouragement goes a long way.

Creating a critical environment will hinder your team's growth. The last thing you want is for your staff to fear your decision-making. Fear will hinder your team's growth in creativity and development. It creates unnecessary stress, which can develop into illnesses, and poor behavior traits. Acknowledge what opportunities are present and what corrections need to be made with your employee, and trust that they're mature and responsible enough to make the necessary changes. If changes are not made, follow your company's corrective plan, but that doesn't mean you have or keep a personal grudge against that person.

Discussion 4.0

How can a leader ensure another employee that they aren't holding a grudge?

Effects of not forgiving

There's nothing good that can come from not forgiving; it turns into bitterness. Our bodies are not designed to hold on to pain; the body will turn on itself and destroy itself from the inside out if it continues to be in pain. It's a silent killer.

Unfortunately, people don't realize how not forgiving can have you stuck in the past. Not only will it paralyze you with fear with past pain and trauma, but it doesn't allow you to dream and walk in your truth. Forgiveness allows you to be free to live for today. Every person has experienced a level of dysfunction in their lives which as resulted with some level of bad behavior. Hurt people hurt people and with unforgiveness the saga continues, knowingly or unknowingly.

We talk in lesson two about how stress effects the body. I can speak from personal experience how I watch close family members hold grudges for years over childhood experiences not allowing them to enjoy the basic joys of life such as; family reunions, birthday parties or just a fun Sunday together. They made a choice to keep reminding themselves of the past and not living for today. What a disappointing life to experience. What if, we intentionally learned from past mistakes and moved forward with life without the fear of being hurt again, because ultimately that's the real reason why you are choosing to not forgive. You can make excuses and say, "no it's because they did "such and such" but remember you forgiving them does not get them off the hook from hurting you; instead, it frees your thoughts, energy, and time from the past offense. No one is suggesting you go have coffee with this person, you may never be close to them again. The key is to understand all forgiveness is self-forgiveness. Decide to no longer allow another person to control your thoughts, which will determine your behavior. Learn to let it go, for your own physical and mental health.

Karen Swartz, M.D from John Hopkins says the following about not forgiving.

> "There is an enormous physical burden to being hurt and disappointed," says Karen Swartz, M.D., director of the Mood Disorders Adult Consultation Clinic at The Johns Hopkins Hospital. Chronic anger puts you into a fight-or-flight mode, which results in numerous changes in heart rate, blood pressure, and immune response. Those changes increase the risk of depression, heart disease, and diabetes, among other conditions. Forgiveness, however, calms stress levels, leading to improved health."

> "Forgiveness is not just about saying the words, it is an active process in which you make a conscious decision to let

go of negative feelings, whether the person deserves it or not," Swartz says. "As you release the anger, resentment, and hostility, you begin to feel empathy, compassion, and sometimes affection for the person who wronged you."

"Studies have found that some people are just naturally more forgiving. Consequently, they tend to be more satisfied with their lives and to have less depression, anxiety, stress, anger, and hostility. However, people who hang on to grudges are more likely to experience severe depression, post-traumatic stress disorder and other health conditions. But that doesn't mean that they can't train themselves to act in healthier ways. In fact, 62 percent of American adults say they need more forgiveness in their personal lives, according to a survey by the nonprofit Fetzer Institute."

http://www.hopkinsmedicine.org/health/healthy_aging/healthy_connect
ions/forgiveness-your-health-depends-on-it

Discussion 4.1

Do you have any ill feelings towards a coworker? If yes, how is this affecting you physically or mentally?

Notes

Lesson

5

Lesson 5

HOW DO I FORGIVE?

- ✓ LOOK AT THE INNOCENT
- ✓ MAKE A DECISION
- ✓ REMEMBER YOUR GOAL
- ✓ FORGIVENESS IS FOR YOU

Look at the innocent.

As we discussed throughout the book, everyone comes with a past. This past has become a part of the ingredients that form our character. When someone hurts us, because ultimately that's what happens, we must look at the innocence behind it and understand this behavior was taught. Even liars and manipulators were taught. Forgive the inner child. When people know better, they do better. They honestly don't know how their actions affect the people around them.

Make a decision.

Once you get an understanding of innocence, you can decide to forgive. That doesn't mean you'll be going to lunch with them next week, but you have moved on. You see that person for who they are, you're not passing judgment upon them, but now you know how to deal with this personally.

Remember your goal.

Remember your purpose, dream, and goal; that's where your focus needs to be. Holding on to grudges will only delay your process and distract you. Let it go; it's not worth it and not connected to your purpose. Ask yourself, is holding on to this offense helping me achieve my goal?

Discipline is at the core.
With the understanding that our past experiences shape our behavior. We must learn to unlearn behavior and keep learning new healthier ways of living. If holding grudges, not admitting when your wrong were behaviors demonstrated or accepted around you as a child it will be difficult to forgive. You must learn new behavior which will take discipline and consistency to truly change.

Forgiveness is for you.
Understand that no one is perfect, and forgiveness doesn't mean you'll immediately start feeling better, or you can salvage that relationship. Instead, you've decided to no longer allow that experience to control your emotions and future. Forgive yourself for holding on to it and preventing promotions or opportunities; with your new awareness, new opportunities will come.

Lastly and so important, remember the golden rule, "Do unto others, as you would have them do unto you." We want to be forgiven for mistakes we've made, but we are not quick to do the same for others. The next time you're about to make a judgement towards someone, think about a time in your life when you failed big time and how you felt when someone didn't let it go. Learn and develop from that, don't repeat the cycle of not forgiving, and understand the power of FORGIVENESS.

At the end of the day, "F" it; forgive to remain free!

Discussion 5.0

- Think of a time where someone did not let go of something you did in the past; how did it make you feel?

- Are you repeating this behavior towards someone in your life today?

- Can you make a decision to forgive and let go?

- Can you think of a person in your workplace that you need to forgive? Are you willing to let it go, and open up new opportunities in your future?

____

____

____

____

____

Notes

About the Author

Amanda Hill is a wife, mother, working high fashion model, NPC (National Physique Committee) Bikini competitor, an author, and has an amazing corporate career as a Sr. Account Manager for a leading healthcare vendor. She has earned a bachelor's degree in Business Administration, a Certification in Project Management, and studied in the field of Lean Six Sigma.

In life, Amanda has discovered that her passion is living a healthy life and encouraging others to do the same. Through her company, Keys to Balance, she teaches people how to live a balanced life, physically, spiritually, and mentally through her life experiences. Amanda used to be afraid to discuss her past traumas; now, she wears them as a crown. Amanda is also the author of a book entitled "The Faith Within Me: Lessons Learned, Through Times of Trial.

9 7 9 8 2 1 8 0 6 5 5 6 0